W9-ACM-569

The Art of Growing

MINIATURE TREES,

Plants
and Landscapes

JAPANESE BONSAI AND BONKEI
ADAPTED TO
WESTERN CONDITIONS

The Art of Growing **MINIATUR**

by Tatsuo Ishim

Author of **THE ART OF FLOWER ARRANGEMENT**
THE ART OF DRIFTWOOD AND DRIED ARRANGEMENTS
THE ART OF PLANT AND DRIFTWOOD ARRANGEMENTS

JAPANESE BONSAI AND BONKEI
ADAPTED TO
WESTERN CONDITIONS

REES, *Plants and Landscapes*

HEFFER & SONS LTD.
MBRIDGE

Dedication:

For Alice and Proc

Table of Contents

Foreword

This book offers to the gardener, the plant lover, the hobbyist, the flower arranger something more than a discovery in gardening. It offers a discovery in living . . . a new goal, a deeply satisfying relationship with nature. Actually, this is a discovery only for Westerners, for Americans. In Japan it is one of the most ancient and respected of the household arts. It is called *Bonsai*.

Until very recently *bonsai* was quite unknown in America. If you asked for a book on *bonsai* in any American library you would get a polite look and a headshake. In the last few years one or two books published in Japan have become available, and quite recently, a first American book. All of these are worthwhile, but none of them adequately covers the how-to-do-it of *bonsai* in photographs, and none explores the different ways in which the *bonsai* idea can be adapted and simplified to suit American ideas, American tastes . . . and American patience or lack of it! (In Japan a *bonsai* is often started by a man . . . to be enjoyed by his grandson 50 years later. Not every American feels he has this much time and not every American is so sure his grandson will be interested!)

What is this discovery? What is *bonsai*?
Superficially, a *bonsai* is a miniature living tree (or shrub or even vine) grown in a shallow plant container.
In Japanese eyes, however, a *bonsai* is much more than this; *bonsai* is an art form which has developed and matured over the course of eight centuries.
The miniature *bonsai* tree is not just an ingeniously dwarfed plant grown with great skill to great age in a handful of soil. Instead, the tree is truly the art-creation of its owner. It is not just a tiny tree, it is a landscape in miniature. (Sometimes the fancier prefers to grow *bonkei*, which are gardens in miniature.) The *bonsai* tree is old (5 years, 10 years, 60 years) but looks much older; the idea is to create in time a genuine ancient, in miniature. A Japanese will find a young tree that reminds him of another tree he may have seen on a hillside, in a field, near a lake, or on a mountainside. He will plant this small tree in a container, striving to make it develop in small scale as completely as the larger tree he admired grew full scale in nature. What he does is to restrict root growth (with the container), carefully pinching leaves, pruning and training the top to conform to the limited root system.

American interest in miniature trees, miniature landscapes, and miniature gardens first began to take hold in the years right after World War II. The start was slow, but it is picking up speed at an astonishing rate today.

In many American cities one can see *bonsai* displays in local botanical gardens. Nurseries and florists are displaying *bonsai*, selling *bonsai* containers, offering young seedlings for sale for training as *bonsai*.

The interest is here. But the traditional Japanese *bonsai* technique is slow, tedious, and calls for great delicacy and great skill.

This is the reason for my book. Why not a simplified *bonsai*? Why not results the first year? Why not a book that tells of an easier, quicker way to grow miniature trees—to create miniature landscapes?

With such an idea in mind, I went to work planting, growing, training, pruning, potting and repotting. I have had the wise counsel of many distinguished growers of *bonsai*. Not all of my experimental efforts were successful, but the successes have been very exciting, not only to me but to many who have grown *bonsai* only in the ancient way.

Here, then, is our discovery—a simplified approach to growing miniature trees and miniature landscapes. All photographs in this book are my own.

T. I.

San Francisco

Bonsai: Centuries old in Japan—
very new in America

The art of dwarfing trees in a small container is centuries old. Its beginnings are obscure: the earliest known Japanese examples are pictured on a celebrated scroll which dates back to the early thirteenth century. Yet this was certainly not the beginning of this garden art form. In China, for centuries, certain ornamental trees traditionally had been grown in pots or containers for decorative use in gardens. Small pot-grown flowering trees were forced into bloom for the New Year season.

The technique of growing small trees in small containers crossed the East China Sea sometime before the thirteenth century, a part of the broad stream of cultural ideas moving from the mainland to the Japanese islands, a stream that

This 21-inch *bonsai* is the size preferred by many connoisseurs. It is a juniper which has been growing for three-hundred-and-thirty-five years.

An unusual *bonsai* of bamboo.

Carved volcanic rock makes an "ancient" setting for this black pine *bonsai*.

brought to Japan the Buddhist religion and the Kanji characters that compose Japan's written language.

In Japan the art of creating miniature container-grown landscapes changed slowly as the centuries passed. Skilled growers learned and taught their sons the technique of training trunk and branch, pruning roots, pinching tips and buds, preparing and renewing soils. Until fairly recent times, however, the *bonsai* art remained a specialist's art. Then, in the last century, *bonsai* art suddenly took on a broad popularity. Amateur growers by the hundreds and thousands took up the art and studied its technique. *Bonsai* exhibitions became popular, even commonplace. The age-old techniques were discussed, written down, classified. In this century the art of the miniature tree continued to gain popular appeal. The recent war only caused a pause in the development of *bonsai*. Since the war, interest in the little trees has swept ahead in Japan. *Bonsai* clubs are numerous, *bonsai* exhibitions well attended. Thousands of Americans, stationed in Japan, have admired the lovely, ancient-looking trees, and have asked about the creative art they represent.

Now, the idea has made its way across the Pacific and has taken first root in America. Already there are *bonsai* nurseries, *bonsai* clubs, even direct mail advertisers of "genuine *bonsai*." (Most of the ads, in the author's observation, are unfortunate; even so, their wide circulation has helped to confirm the growing interest in miniature trees. Actually, the advertised offerings in the cases the author has checked are not true *bonsai* at all.)

[11]

Not just a tree—a miniature landscape

Before we discuss how the *bonsai* idea can be simplified, it is wise to understand the nature of the authentic, painstakingly created Japanese *bonsai*.

The goal of the *bonsai*-grower is the creation of a natural landscape, usually dominated by a tree ancient in feeling . . . all of the composition in miniature. The grower-artisan works patiently with a sensitive eye for his natural composition. He works to achieve harmony. All the elements of his composition—trunk, roots, branches, leaves, perhaps blossoms and fruit—must be in proportion.

Since the trunk is the most important element, let us consider it first. A trunk too slim or bent into an unnatural shape will not do, neither will a trunk too long for the mass of the *bonsai*.

On the other hand, should a trunk split, become gnarled, decayed—with the resulting impression of old age surviving the elements—then its character will contribute to the authentic feeling of the complete composition.

Careful selection of plants with small leaves and blossoms, judicious pruning and pinching—these also are essential if you are to produce the happy balance you desire.

Naturalness is the rule always, and the properly developed *bonsai* will be pleasing from any viewpoint. Give the plant plenty of sunlight, fresh air and, after it is well established in its container, limited moisture. Treat it always, however, with tender care—just enough discipline.

Deciduous trees make excellent subjects because of their changing beauty through the seasons. But the pruner's artistry and sympathy with nature is important if you are to have a well designed trunk with branches and twigs in graceful proportion. Many coniferous evergreens are favorites also, in part because they grow naturally in shapes that suggest the never ending struggle with nature for survival.

The exposed portion of the root must also contribute to the total impression. Above all, the rootage should convey a feeling of stability. This is why seedlings grown in pots usually make the best miniatures.

Trees grown from cuttings have a more difficult adjustment. Trees transplanted from rocky ground may also have a difficult adjustment, but their root-systems already have adapted themselves to spartan conditions and for this reason, such trees make promising *bonsai* subjects.

What kinds of trees should be used?

In America we have been growing potted trees for many years, but we have not called them *bonsai*. While the Japanese container is shallow, we have used taller containers, and just as Japanese ideas and plant materials vary from ours, so have the styles and shapes of our container-grown plants been vastly different.

This fifteen-year-old boxwood stands about 15 inches tall.

Wherever you live, it is easy to find plants suitable for container growing—in miniature. Nurseries provide a large selection, and the advantages of buying your trees from a nursery are numerous. Such trees are usually root bound. Wide choice of shape is possible. The trees are previously adapted to your particular local climate. A tree or shrub already in a pot or can is already arrested in its growth. Controlling its shape will be easier; much of the hard work has already been done for you by the nursery.

Since the beauty and charm of any *bonsai* comes with increasing age, it is wise to choose a long lived plant with a rugged temperament. Usually such plants can take the severe adjustments required in the dwarfing procedures. As always, if you let nature be your guide, you aren't likely to make a wrong choice.

Consider the pine—the "king of trees." In nature, when soil and climate are right, it grows into a magnificent specimen. But poor soil and a harsh climate do not defeat the pine. You can discover pine clinging firmly to a rocky mountain ledge in defiance of the elements. See the coastal pine deeply rooted in a sand dune, bent low against the sea wind. Consider the pines serenely at home on arid, sun-baked hillsides, or fighting for existence on rocky high-mountain slopes. The pines are "natural" then for the miniature tree grower. And of the many species, the short needled are most adaptable to graceful miniature effects.

The Japanese white pine (*Pinus parviflora*) is one of the best choices among the pines. Also called the five needled pine, its small needles and delicate proportions make it a superior subject.

Other popular varieties are the Japanese black pine (*P. thumbergii*), the Japanese red pine (*P. densiflora*), the Austrian pine or Black pine (*P. nigra*), and the popular Mugho pine (*P. mugo mughus*). Many other pines have been dwarfed into beautiful form, but some have needles too large in scale for effective miniature display.

Or you may choose for your *bonsai* one of many other easily adapted coniferous evergreens—juniper, spruce, cedar, fir. Many of the oldest and most distinguished Japanese *bonsai* are Sargent's juniper. (*Juniperus chinensis sargenti.*)

The hardy Yeddo (sometimes Yezo or Yesso) spruce (*Rica jezoensis*) is a near perfect subject for miniature landscapes. Not only are its proportions excellent, but it is quite easy to grow and train.

Most popular with the Japanese of the flowering trees is the *ume* or Japanese apricot (*Prunus mume*). The *ume,* of which there are said to be more than 200 distinguishable varieties, is easily trained and its dainty fragrant blossoms are a perfect adornment for the miniature tree.

The *ume* is especially treasured by the Japanese because its early blossoming indoors is so in contrast to the wintry winds outside.

The *bonsai* of flowering cherry is valued for its shapeliness as well as for its profuse and colorful blossoms. Unlike the Japanese apricot, the cherry is quite difficult to grow and train.

Among deciduous foliage trees one has an almost endless choice. Particularly popular are the small leafed Japanese maples. The leaves range in color from light green to red. The hawthorne, the quince, the Japanese elm, the liquidambar, the ginkgo, the beech, the Japanese birch—all are favored subjects for miniatures.

So are other quite different plants. Azaleas and camellias make excellent subjects. Chrysanthemums grown in cascade style give you *bonsai* effects in a matter of weeks. Boston ivy (*Parthenocissus tricuspidata*) and small leafed Boston ivy (*P. t. veitchii*) can be trained into interesting shrub form. The Japanese boxwood (*Buxus microphylla japanica*) is not a favorite of the *bonsai* expert, but in my experience there are few plants so easy to train in miniature.

Too many choices? Not really. Consider the effect you wish to create—then choose a subject that promises you success.

When the time comes to begin your first miniature, study carefully the photographs in this book. They provide visual guidance to supplement the descriptive text.

How the Japanese classify their miniature trees

There are four size groups of miniature trees:

Mame-Bonsai: These are the "baby" *bonsai,* never taller than 5 inches to 6 inches. They became popular about one hundred years ago. Sake cups (tiny pottery cups without handles) are sometimes used for containers for these tiny trees. Three to five *Mame-bonsai* can be lined up on the palm of the hand. These little fellows are difficult to grow. They are really a discipline and a delight for the very few.

Ko-Bonsai: These 6- to 12-inch trees are probably the most popular size. Like all *bonsai,* they must be in proportion to the container. If the container is 2 inches high, many *bonsai* cultivators believe the tree should measure about 6 inches from soil level to tree top.

Chiu-Bonsai: Many people prefer this size—up to 2 feet in height—because of the variety of the containers available and because this is an easy size to train.

Dai-Bonsai: These are the large *bonsai*—over 2 feet in height. It usually takes two or more people to carry such a tree. The name in Japanese means large; therefore, if two people have to lift a *bonsai,* it is a *Dai-bonsai.*

The Japanese also classify their little trees by shape and style: *Chokkan* designates the erect, natural looking tree; *shakon*—slanting trunk, *hankon*—gnarled trunk, and *kengai*—drooping trunk. *Kengai* also denotes the cascading style. Another classification is by the number of trunks. A cluster of trees growing together, such as three or more on one side of the container, and perhaps two smaller ones on the other side, is given the name of *Yose-ue.* A *yose-ue* might resemble a small group or groups of trees growing in a field. There can be as many trees as you wish to use. Other styles are *kabumono*—two or more trunks from one stump, *Ne-tsuranari*—several trunks from one root, *Ishi-tsuki*—trunk growing from a stone clasped by the roots.

The miniature garden or landscape is termed *Bonkei.*

In *bonsai* the miniature landscape effect is achieved by the tree or trees and the soil or soil and stone. The Japanese also make *bonkei* which are miniature gardens. In *bonkei,* trees, rocks, grass, moss, tiny plants or vines, small models of houses, bridges, and small figures of people are combined to make a natural looking scene in a container. *Bonkei* is not as popular as *bonsai* in Japan, but the *bonkei* idea offers endless possibilities for the American who wants to work with a variety of ideas and materials.

Bonsai—in the open garden

American gardeners have often asked me about the place of *bonsai* in the over-all picture of Japanese gardening. They also have wondered if the *bonsai* idea is limited to container plantings. Let's see if I can explain this relationship.

Tradition guides the hand of the Japanese gardener, just as it guides the hand of the Japanese *bonsai* grower. Over the centuries the private garden in Japan has evolved as a serene composition in stone, water, and planting—a restful scene to look out upon, an invitation to repose and quiet contemplation. The Japanese garden usually is small in scale and exquisite in its proportions.

Bonsai in Japan bears about the same relationship to over-all Japanese gardening as pot gardening in America does to the total American garden scheme. In America we use pot-grown plants to "furnish" our terraces, to provide seasonal change. Our gardens are usually informal and large scale, and so, often, are our container plants. In Japan the training of one *bonsai* is as formal a business as the design of a complete garden.

The *bonsai* are always container plants, of course. Being outdoor plants, they often have their own showcase within the garden—a series of display benches where the grower can care for their wants and show them off to his friends.

Some American gardeners have asked me, "Can't I grow *bonsai* in the open ground? I'd like to have an intimate corner in my garden with all plants in miniature. Don't the Japanese ever do this?"

Such a garden of miniatures does not have a place in Japanese gardening. Nor can you grow *bonsai* in the open ground; the container is necessary to restrict growth. But there is no reason why you cannot have an intimate outdoor garden of miniature plants if you wish. Here is one way to achieve such an intimate garden: Select a suitable spot, sheltered from the wind, perhaps along one side of your terrace. Build a low backdrop of natural wood fencing (cedar or cypress or redwood), or put in an informal hedge planting as your backdrop. In a space perhaps 3 or 4 feet wide in front of your backdrop create a raised planting bed about 12 inches above ground level. To contain the raised bed, build a low masonry wall, or build a wooden wall using 2x12 treated planks secured by 4x4 treated posts with a 2x6 treated cap.

In the raised bed you can arrange a series of *bonsai* trees and shrubs right in their containers, creating the effect of a miniature landscape or garden scene. If you like, you can sink the containers to their rims in soil, leaf mold, or peat moss. Between them and behind them you can experiment with stones placed to suggest rock outcroppings and perhaps a stony mountain background. Between containers, if you wish, you can plant moss.

Your *bonsai* culture will go on just as if your plants were above ground. You will water them and feed them in the regular way. When necessary you will lift your containers for repotting, then return them to their places in the raised planting bed. You will need to watch your watering carefully as the sunken pots will dry out more slowly than pots above ground, and so should get by with less frequent watering. You also should lift your pots about twice a year and prune away any roots growing through the drainage holes.

Without looking at the container, can you tell which is the miniature tree?

The place to begin your study of miniature trees is out of doors—on a walk in the country, in the mountains, along the coastline, in your own garden.

If you are a camera fan, make snapshots of the full-size trees that interest you. Study their form, the weathering, the shape of trunk and branch.

Study the photographs here. Don't look at the containers. See how similar trees are in full scale and in miniature? Here is the heart of *bonsai*.

The trees you see in nature

Every tree you see has a characteristic size and form that is natural to it—born from within its original seed, modified over the years by soil and climate.

A tree struggles to adjust to its environment. It may grow taller or shorter. Its branches may become less symmetrical and even misshapen. The size and color of its leaves will be affected. If it is a fruiting tree, the size, shape and color of the blossoms and the fruit will change. Wind, moisture, sun, soil—all will have their effects.

Four "digger" pines. Stately, strong, uncrowded; their symmetry gives an impression of quietude and peace.

A twisted deciduous oak atop the western slope of a California hillside. Winds off the Pacific Ocean have bent it eastward since its childhood.

A Monterey cypress. This tree tells a thrilling story of struggles waged against sea winds and waves.

The Japanese took their cue from nature. Observing her countless ways of adjusting to environment, they evolved the *bonsai*—recreation in miniature of nature's effects.

Notice the trees pictured here—growing on the seacoast, in a field, on a windswept hill. Can't you picture similar trees, a scant two feet high, growing in a container on your terrace?

Where will you get your miniature trees?

Should you buy your tree in a nursery or dig it in the country? There are advantages to each.

If you go into the country, you will have a valuable opportunity to observe your bonsai subject in its normal habitat—living and growing as the elements and its own nature command. But you will face difficulties, too. Native trees don't transplant easily.

As a beginner, you would be wise to go to the nursery for your first miniature trees. There you will have your choice of sturdy plants well adjusted to life in a container—roots already conformed to a small space. The tree you buy may already be five years old or older; you will save a lot of time.

At the nursery you will have many choices before you, and there will be many trees more handsome than the one you seek.

The salesman may try to sell you a tree that appears to be well shaped and fast growing—the kind of tree you would buy to plant in your garden. Don't listen to him. The tree best suited for miniature cultivation is just the opposite. The tree you are looking for probably is a tree no one else wants. Because of its stunted, scrawny look, you may get it for very little.

Here are points to keep in mind when you shop in the nursery: Consider the tree's habit in its natural environment. Watch its trunk system. Does it have a large trunk? Is its form unusual? Stunted? Old looking? Are you attracted to it? Does its form interest you? Does the plant's present form lend itself to modification by bending or pruning? What kind of container would best suit it?

If your choice is a deciduous tree, you will want to see it in leaf. Are the leaves small enough to be in good proportion to a dwarf trunk?

The nursery man can help you with advice on transplanting, proper soil, fertilizing, watering, and the kind of exposure your plant prefers. But remember—few nurserymen know much about growing miniature trees. Think over his advice before you follow it.

If you decide to bring your tree from the fields or mountains, dig it in winter to be sure that it is dormant. Your chances of success are greater if you choose a young tree.

Differences in climate and altitude may make it difficult for the tree you dig and bring home. Another hazard will result from the need to cut the deep taproot.

You may find a likely subject high up on a rocky slope. If you do, remember it is best to dig it right after rain. Otherwise, take extra water along and soak the base well before digging. The moisture will help the roots to hold the soil, which should not be disturbed. Leave a ball of soil at least one foot in diameter around the roots—the more, the better. Have a wet sack ready to wrap around roots and soil, and tie it well so that they will not separate.

This juniper in a can is a likely subject for an attractive bonsai.

Discover the possibilities of your subject by bending it this way and that.

As soon as you get home with your tree, dig a hole in a protected spot in your garden in the shade and sheltered from the wind. Then plant it, sack and all. Water it well. A wild tree needs much more care in transplanting than the ordinary nursery tree. Even after transplanting it must become adjusted to the garden atmosphere. Even when you are sure your tree is healthy again (you can tell by the freshness of the leaves) it is wise to wait until a full year has elapsed before transplanting it into a container. Do not rush your transplanting.

The best time to transplant from the mountains or fields is while the tree is dormant—usually from October to April, depending on the location.

The Japanese favor bonsai plants dug from rocky mountainous slopes. These hardy little trees—pine, juniper, cherry, ume—had adjusted to the barren soil and the rigorous climate. They were tough and strong, ready to live a long life in the scant soil in their earthen containers.

But you are far from Japan. Perhaps you have never even seen a genuine bonsai. My best advice to you is to do as the Japanese have done. Get your inspiration from photographs and from effects that please you in nature. Then go to work with whatever materials are close at hand.

Our country has a different culture, landscape, climate from Japan. You can learn much from the Japanese but don't worry if you cannot find the same plants. In the United States there are thousands of fine plants which will develop into beautiful bonsai—with results showing quickly enough to satisfy the most impatient enthusiast.

This hexagonal bonsai container has three drainage holes.

Why is the container so important?

Here is a bit of interesting history on containers—especially bonsai pots. Centuries ago Chinese horticulturists labored to hollow out rocks of different sizes to make containers for their plants. And these "natural" containers did convey the illusion of plants growing in their normal setting—in a field or on a mountainside. Then someone—looking for an easier way, no doubt—discovered that ceramic tile could be shaped and baked into a pot to replace the hollow rock. These first pots were the color of the powdered rock and earth from which they were made. As craftsmen improved their methods, they added beautifully colored glazes and intricate designs.

Next to selecting the tree itself, your choice of container is your most important decision in creating your miniature landscape.

The shape, size, color and material of that container must contribute to the aesthetic harmony of the whole.

If your creation is to be a landscape in miniature, then shouldn't the container suggest brown earth or grey rocks? Other good container colors are off-white and deep red.

The ideal container—hexagonal, dark brown, unglazed pottery—comes in three sizes. The tree you start with will decide the size of your container.

is pottery container's dimensions are similar to original nursery can or pot, so tree's adjust-nt is easier.

Japanese-made containers, like this decorated bonsai container with exterior glaze are available in many different designs.

may find this oval-shaped unglazed terra cotta ainer in chocolate brown useful.

This earthenware pot with exterior glaze comes in several sizes and in several colors.

It is not a good idea to use a brilliantly colored or highly decorated pot for your miniatures. The unity intrinsic to any work of art will be destroyed as tree and container compete for attention.

After learning all you can about your tree and its habits, trust your own judgment regarding the container. Choose what looks good to you, since your work of art should be an expression of yourself. A wood container can well be used. Some such containers have an inside pot. If you have a wood craftsman at home, ask him to try his hand at making you a shallow wood container of cedar, redwood or cypress. Let the wood weather naturally; its weathered color will combine handsomely with your miniature landscape.

Most of the time you can be sure that the trees you buy in a gallon can or 8-inch pot will fit a medium-sized container, perhaps 7 inches wide, 11 inches long, 3 inches deep. Some trees, such as the flowering and fruiting trees and the bamboos, prefer a deep container.

The shape you choose—round, square, oval, hexagonal, free form—depends on your own artistic judgment.

The Japanese feel that the age of the container should also be in harmony with the plant—an old looking, weathered container for an aged tree . . . a fresh, newly baked one for a young tree. Rough textured pottery seems in keeping with vigorous dwarf trees.

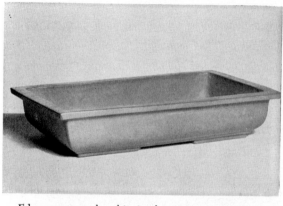

Edge contour makes this simple container interesting.

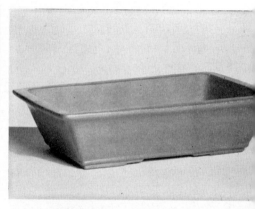

A simple container with severe lines is prac

You may prefer a shallow container sitting on feet.

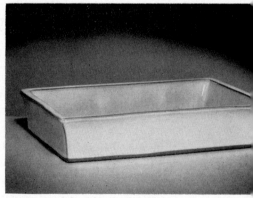

Flower containers can be used for bonsai

The container of this 40-inch-high juniper has five drainage holes.

Your container should have one or several drain holes, depending on its size. These holes permit drainage of excess water, and also admit air to the soil. The holes must never be closed. But neither can they be left wide open because the soil would leak through them. Several kinds of satisfactory covers have been devised. One is simply a square of wire screen of very fine mesh placed well over the hole. Another is a small perforated earthen cup placed upside down over each hole. You can use pieces of a broken pot curved down over the holes.

Fine mesh wire screen, broken clay pot, rocks—any of these is suitable for covering the drain holes.

How to prepare the container

Regardless of the size or kind of tree, the principles for transplanting into a pot are the same. First, cover the drain holes with fine wire mesh, with pieces of broken pot, or with irregular pieces of rock.

Whatever covering you use, be sure that the holes are not plugged up. Water must drain out and air must find its way through the soil.

Next, cover the bottom of your container with a layer of gravel. This will help to hold the soil while permitting water to drain off.

Now, add a layer of sand. Some prefer to mix the sand with gravel.

Next comes a dry layer of your especially prepared soil mix and you are ready to plant your tree. Your soil mix should match as closely as possible the original soil provided to your plant by nature. Some plants do much better in one kind of soil than in another; you can be sure that whatever soil conditions you find in the natural habitat will work for your tree.

...how it's done. Here, as examples, we find wire ...en over one hole, broken piece of pot over the ...er. Next comes a layer of gravel . . . then a layer ...ixed soil.

Use fresh soil, not the soil from the nursery pot. This is important. Your plant will be growing in a minimum of earth; it should be fresh and nourishing if your tree is to get off to a good start.

While many trees can—and do in nature—adjust to almost any kind of soil, your problem is a special one. Your tree must thrive in an absolute minimum of soil. To do so, two soil properties are indispensable: the ability to hold moisture and to admit air.

Generally speaking, coniferous evergreens (pine, spruce, juniper, fir) grow best in a 50-50 mixture of sandy loam and sand, with a small amount of leaf humus or peat moss well mixed in.

The deciduous flowering and broadleafed trees, when well established, prefer less sand and more organic material—say 50% or more sandy loam and clay mixture, 20% or less sand, and the remaining 30% well powdered leaf mold or peat moss.

Some growers prefer to hurry their trees by using a soil mix richer than that nature would provide, but this can be risky.

[29]

How to remove your tree from the nurseryman's can or pot

Ordinarily, the tree you get from the nursery is already in a can or pot. If you are going to transplant it at once, the nurseryman will cut the can for you and you are ready to go, for the moisture around the roots will be just right for transplanting.

If, however, you are going to delay the transplanting, then you will have to cut the can yourself when you are ready, meanwhile watering the plant at proper intervals.

When you are ready to transplant, be sure there is enough moisture around the roots to hold the soil together, but not enough to make it sticky.

If your tree is in a can, use a tin snips to cut the opposite sides, as shown in the photograph. If the can is large, you may have to cut it on all four sides to facilitate removal of roots and soil intact.

Should your tree be in a pot, turn the pot upside down, gently tap the bottom and sides with your hand to loosen the soil from the sides. Sometimes a wooden mallet or stick will help. Do your best to remove roots and soil together.

Turn pot upside down. Knock it gently against a wooden box to loosen the small tree.

Remove plant without disturbing soil around roots.

Water your tree in its pot the day before transplanting.

Cut can away from the tree. Make two or more cuts.

Bend the can away from the root ball.

Lift out tree without disturbing soil near root. Be careful not to cut your hands. (It's a good idea to wear garden gloves.)

From can—to finished product

What miracle has taken place? Not a miracle at all—just a new home for your little tree—a home with a future.

Suddenly your tree is a part of a landscape. Squint your eye and you can almost see it off on the horizon, growing between a cleft in two huge rocks, silhouetted against the sky.

You are on your way. Already here is a landscape in miniature. But it will grow greatly in interest as you train your tree.

Owner—Emyko Kumamoto

How to plant your miniature tree

Once your plant is out of its original container, your job is to remove, in the shade, a good portion of the old soil without injury to the delicate root hairs. A narrow stick, such as a chopstick, is a good tool to use here. Some gardeners I know have whittled their own bonsai tools. Others use a pencil. Remove at least two-thirds of the old soil. (Some experts remove almost all the old soil from flowering and fruit trees.)

Let the natural soil around the tree and the root condition guide you. If you see a lot of roots, it means the roots need fresh soil. Take out about two-thirds of the old soil. If the earth is fresh around the roots, then you need remove only about one-third of the old soil.

If the earth is fresh around the roots, this may be an indication that your tree has been transplanted recently; if so, you do not want to disturb too much of the root hair. In pruning your roots try to cut off all dead, weak and sick-looking roots. It will be fairly simple for you to decide which roots to prune. As you break or cut the roots, the old and dead ones will resemble dried wood or dead branches on a tree.

When your root pruning is finished, place the plant in the container in the desired position. Push it firmly in place, then fill the pot with the dry prepared mixed soil you have ready. Take care to see that the soil reaches all parts of the roots. Moist soil is easy to work with, but you must be very careful, as it may not reach all the roots. Use your narrow stick to assist you. Make sure that the old soil and the new are well bonded, and that the edges are well packed all around. The new soil should be pressed down firmly around the tree. Evergreens and pines require the most pressure, and the broad-leafed, deciduous trees the least. Your tree should now be firmly in place. If it shows signs of wobbling then press down more firmly.

As you transplant, be careful not to cover the tree trunk with soil. Don't worry if you expose upper surfaces of the root to the air; this will help your bonsai adjust to its new container environment.

Now sprinkle your tree and soil gently with a fine spray until the water begins to drain out of all the holes. Natural untreated water from a river or a lake is best for this purpose. If this is difficult to obtain, don't worry, the risk with treated or chlorinated water is not great.

Your bonsai should be carefully sheltered from sun, wind and rain until its roots have become active again—at least two weeks. During this critical period keep the soil moist by sprinkling. After two weeks or so begin to adjust your miniature tree to the elements again. Give it hours at first, with consideration for the plant's natural leanings toward sun or shade. When the proper adjustment is completed, sun, wind, rain or cold should not harm it. Your bonsai is an outdoor plant; you

Gently remove old soil from roots.

Place tree in desired position in container and press down firmly.

Add the soil, tamping down well.

Push the soil down around plant with a narrow stick. Add more soil as necessary.

Press down firmly with your hands, paying special attention to the edges. Water well.

Here is the finished product, with decorative rocks added.

should treat it as such. Exposure to all the elements as nearly as the natural habitat provides is essential if your tree is to be vigorous, healthy and disease-resistant. On the other hand, too much exposure to very strong wind or the summer sun may damage your plant. Consider the environment nature has given it and reproduce this as nearly as possible, remembering that the *bonsai* may require just a little more protection from the extremes than a full-size tree.

Transplanting from one container to another

How can you tell when your bonsai needs transplanting? Here are five clues to watch for:

The tree looks unbalanced.

The tree apparently has no style.

The tree needs to be cut back to its original shape.

The roots and soil are pushing up out of the container.

The tree appears to be losing its vigor.

Generally speaking, the dormant time just before your bonsai tree starts to grow is the best time for transplanting. Coniferous evergreens should be transplanted every four or five years; the flowering and fruiting trees about once a year; elm and maple every two years.

Miniature Landscapes

Here is what you can quickly achieve by following the directions just given:

Whether your tree came from the nursery or from the mountains or fields, planting it in its container is done in the same manner. You might use different mixed soil for different trees, and perhaps secondary material such as rocks and moss, smaller trees, tiny figures, to create a more realistic or detailed landscape effect.

Owner: Harold Iwamasa

This colorful shrub, pyracantha, makes an interesting miniature because of its blossoms in spring and bright red berries in autumn. The small berries are in excellent scale with the dwarfed trunk.

An older-looking miniature. Notice the contrast with the bonsai on the opposite page. What you see is only the illusion of age. Although this tree was planted in the same way, the rocks make it seem to be growing on a rocky cliff. The heavy trunk adds to its mature appearance.

A spruce—from the nursery

You might run across a spruce this size on a mountain side, yet this one actually came from the nursery. The arrangement of the rocks gives it a sturdy, weathered appearance. The short needles help in creating the illusion of a forest giant. Small in scale, they are in good proportion to the trunk.

This spruce is *Picea nudiformis japonica*. Many other variants of the popular Norway spruce make good miniature subjects.

A pine—from the mountains

Actually from the mountains, this tree makes a sharp contrast with the spruce on the opposite page. Its large trunk and unusual shape suggest an ancient tree. There is no mistaking the feeling it gives of having struggled to grow on a mountain ridge. This is a Tamarack pine.

Spreading wide—from a horizontal container

What makes this miniature mountain cherry so beautiful is the built-up soil in its shallow container and the well distributed small leaves. Notice that the tree grows from one side of the container. Notice, too, the sweeping arch of the trunk at the right.

Reaching high—from a vertical container

(Opposite) Everything in this design reaches upwards. Notice the lone rock, the tall container, and the redwood itself (*Sequoia sempervirens*). This miniature is five years old and just 15 inches tall.

The straight branch.

The branch wired and bent, thus made shorter.

Wiring can be used to make a curved branch, a wide or narrow branch or to hold branches together.

How to shape your tree with wire

The purpose in wiring is to make a shorter, smaller tree, and to shape the branches so that they will be in balance and present a more interesting shape. Wiring also enables you to change the direction of the tree, or any part of the tree with which you may not be satisfied.

Years ago in Japan a fad for grotesque and unnatural tree forms was popular. Happily, it is outmoded today. In this book I am not suggesting that you distort your trees. You train them to achieve a *natural* appearance.

The best time to wire and shape your tree is in the springtime when it has just started growing. Actually, you may wire it at any time, but you will achieve faster and better results if you rely on nature and her seasons. While dormant the tree naturally won't change as much or as fast; in winter it is more hardened and not flexible. The suppleness is missing and there is a chance of breaking or snapping a branch.

Wire comes in many different sizes; you must judge the type of wire by the size of your tree trunk and branches. A thick or medium-size tree trunk and heavy branches call for a stronger wire than a small, light tree with small branches. Once you have wired the trunk or branches, the wire must be strong enough to hold them exactly as you have shaped them. If the wire is not strong enough and should slip for even an inch or two, the shape will change and your original idea will be lost.

You start to wire by first anchoring the wire in the soil near the root. Then you wind the wire upward, gently but firmly. Do not have the wire too tight as it might cut into the bark. Also, if you don't leave some space between the wire and trunk, it will not bend. After the wire is wound upward to the spot you want shaped, cut the wire and secure it firmly to the trunk. Then bend to any shape you desire. Only wire the parts of the trunk or branches where the shape is to be changed.

You may wire a branch at any point you like. There are two methods: *One:* Twist the wire around the branch as you did the trunk and bend to desired shape. *Two:* Anchor wire to the trunk of tree and pull the branch over as far as you want, and secure wire to branch. This method also serves to widen spaces between trunk and branches, or to make them narrow, or to hold one branch in place while another is being changed in shape.

A juniper wired before shaping. Note that the wire is coiled loosely around the trunk.

The same juniper after shaping.

Hold the base of trunk firmly as you begin to reshape the tree.

Finish the job, taking special care not to disturb the roots in the pot.

Wire your tree to give it a better shape, to make it shorter, to make the trunk or branches grow in a desired direction—to make your whole composition work as you have visualized it.

While a natural effect is your goal, this certainly does not mean that you should produce a perfectly symmetrical bonsai. Symmetry, indeed, rarely occurs in nature.

Japanese horticulturists, recognizing that nature's beauty is more truly asymmetrical, have worked to achieve beautiful balance while seeming to violate all of its principles.

How long should the wire remain? That depends on the tree. Some will require a year or longer; some will have permanently assumed their new shape in less than a year. In any case, it usually is wise to leave the wire in place through one winter season.

How can you tell when to remove the wire? Make a test. Uncoil the wire, and if your tree stays in the shape as when wired, and does not try to straighten out toward its original shape, then the wire may be removed permanently, or until you wish to reshape. As you unwind the wire, cut it about every eight inches. This keeps the wire from getting too long and makes the task easier.

Cut here.   Do not cut here.

Cut here.   Do not cut here.

How to shape by pruning and pinching

Pruning is the method you use to encourage your tree to take and maintain the desired shape. Pruning should be done in the springtime. Most people do their pruning at the same time they are wiring the tree.

When pruning, make your cuts clean, leaving no remnant of the trunk or branch you have removed to spoil your design.

The fruit and flower bearing trees are treated much as their orchard-growing cousins—all overgrown parts should be cut off as soon as the blossoming period is over.

If your bonsai is a normally broad-leafed deciduous tree, then the number of branches must be kept limited and in an artistic form. The leaves themselves can be made smaller by pinching them off. Newer and smaller ones will then form. The strongest of these, too, are pinched off, forcing the dormant buds to produce even smaller leaves.

Growing branches can also be cut back to the dormant buds, if so desired, and the new growth will have smaller leaves.

Pines and other evergreens will limit their growth and develop more branches if the new green tips on each branch are pinched back, leaving just a bit of the new green behind.

Some evergreens continue to put forth new shoots throughout the growing season; these should be removed whenever they appear, if the original shape of your tree is to be kept. However, some gardeners prefer to let these new shoots grow, thereby changing direction and form.

The leaves or needles themselves may be removed, one by one, to improve the appearance of your bonsai.

How to change form
by wiring and pruning

This young juniper is planted in a container without holes. Place the piece of driftwood near the root to add interest. Use wire and your pruning shears to change the form of your juniper.

The juniper looked like this at first. The arrangement was pleasing but we thought a different and better effect was possible.

Here is the result of quite a lot of trimming. Wire was used to change the direction of some of the branches.

Further pruning and wiring produced this effect.

You can change form at any time

It is better to shape your tree in the spring, but if it is a healthy specimen you actually can change form in almost any season. If you get a new idea, don't be afraid to reshape your tree.

The important thing is to watch the health of your tree; feed, water, and repot as needed. Then you can pinch and prune almost at will.

The tree as it comes from the nursery.

Shaping is not really very difficult

A change of total effect or a change in shape is easily done. As you live with your bonsai, your imagination will suggest ways in which it can be improved. Maybe it will be only a change in the position of the tree in its container. Maybe it will mean rewiring to change the directions of the tree's growth.

Pruning neatens and dramatizes the natural lines or "motion" of your tree.

The plant slanting slightly to the right.

The center branch bent to the left and held with wi

The top left branch here seemed a little too long.   See what a difference it made to prune this one branch.

A small change often makes the critical difference in the final appearance of the miniature tree. Compare the two photographs above. They are almost identical —but not quite. The difference is at the upper left. One small clip with the pruning shears and suddenly everything changes. The tree is more interesting.

What else—besides your tree?

A tree alone is often not enough if you are to create a realistic landscape in miniature. You will need to use secondary materials.

You may want to use moss—ordinary garden moss, Irish moss, or baby tears. In addition to beautifying your over-all setting, moss helps to keep your topsoil in place and to hold in the moisture.

You also may use odd-shaped or unusual rocks which help create a natural environment that complements your tree. You may wish to recreate a favorite scene in which trees grow out of rocks on a cliff or on a mountainside. Try to find just the right pieces at home to set off your tree to its best advantage, to achieve a free natural look.

You may want to use figurines—perhaps a small cow, if you decide on a pastoral or field scene; a tiny bridge, mill, fence or house, if you prefer a more complete or detailed landscape or miniature garden effect. As you use secondary materials, try to keep everything in proportion. Rocks should balance with the trunk and branches. Small grasses, weeds, or mosses may be planted under the larger tree, or trees. Moss helps produce an aged effect. Be sure your figurines are in good scale with the over-all arrangement.

How to care for your trees

Except for occasional display days inside the house, your little trees should live out of doors. Where? Usually it is wise to choose a location having sun part of the day and shade part of the day.

The best way to water is to simulate a gentle rain by using a sprinkling can with many holes. If you use a hose, attach a fine spray to it and keep the pressure low. People who have many bonsai find the hose a timesaver. Water both the tree and the soil. You want to keep dust off the leaves and you want the tree to absorb much of its needed moisture through needles and leaves. The best time to water is in the early morning or late afternoon. If the sun is too hot, it may burn the leaves when they are wet.

Your tree will adjust to the weather in your location. It will need less water in winter than in summer. If your summer days are sometimes very hot, you may need to water your plant at least twice a day. If it gets extremely cold in winter your tree will need less water. Check the soil dampness. Learn to use your own judgment about when to water.

Your tree will not suffer from an occasional indoor visit of two or three days. Some gardeners use their miniature trees as a centerpiece on the dinner table instead of a flower arrangement. While your trees are in the house, guard them against dryness.

If your winters mean ice and freezing weather, it is wise to water in the morning so that all water will be absorbed before nightfall. The tree itself will adjust to your weather and should remain unharmed. In freezing weather, however, a container may crack and the roots freeze. You can avoid this by placing straw, hay or similar material over and around your containers.

If you leave town for a few days, it is wise to place your tree in a shady spot, on the ground, and water very thoroughly. The tree will then remain safe for several days.

Fertilizing is fairly simple, but it must not be overdone. An overfertilized tree will put on unwanted growth; your main concern is to keep your tree a miniature. Liquid fertilizer is a good choice. I prefer an organic fertilizer; diluted liquid manure or fish emulsion are both good. Two well spaced feedings in the summer and one in early spring should take care of your tree for the year.

A well tended miniature tree will seldom have diseases or insects. Daily watering and spraying usually prevent these troubles.

If the tree has been neglected, insects may appear. In this case the best thing to do is resume the daily watering and spraying routine. If insects are found, try to kill them by hand. As a last resort use an all-purpose spray. Follow the manufacturer's instructions exactly in mixing your spray solution.

No special equipment, other than what you probably already have around the house, is required to grow miniature trees. Some narrow sticks for planting, a wire cutter, pruning shears and a sprinkling can designed to reproduce a gentle shower are the only equipment you need.

How to plant variegated juniper, step by step

Why does this tree make good bonsai material?

It comes from the nursery. Transplanting is easy.
Its size is right and it is well shaped.
It has a large trunk in proportion to the rest of the tree.

Do your transplanting in the shade. The sun can dry and perhaps kill some of the roots. As you work, never allow the roots to become dry.

Variegated juniper, unpotted.

The tree planted in its container and ready to grow.

Use chopsticks or a narrow stick to remove earth from around roots.

Place the tree in a well-balanced location in the container.

Careful and thoughtful consideration should go into the choice of your container. After you have selected your tree, study its shape, size, color and proportions. Consider all of these things in choosing the container for your particular tree. If you like, make a rough sketch, visualizing the over-all arrangement, paying attention to the harmonizing of size, balance, and feeling.

Container chosen, prepare it with wire screen or broken pieces of pot over the drain holes and add your layer of gravel. Now mix your soil. For the juniper pictured here, I used a mixture of one-third sand, one-third natural soil, one-third leaf mold.

You have now reached the point of deciding the exact spot in which to place the tree in the container. Which part of the tree should face the front? Would the tree look better on one side, toward the center, or just a little off center? If you do not like your first decision, experiment with others. Improvement will become apparent as you work.

Location decided, you are ready to cut the can or tap the pot holding your tree. Pull apart; take the tree and roots from the can or slip the root ball from the pot. Hold the trunk of the tree with one hand and remove about three-fourths of the soil, using narrow tools such as the chopsticks shown here. The portion removed will depend on the tree, roots and container. The tree may take quite a beating (this juniper did), but if it is sturdy it will be able to take it. Some trees are more fragile than others; work as delicately as you can.

Next, place the tree in the container in the spot you have selected and see how it looks. If the tree does not stand up as you would wish, or if it stands too high, remove more soil until it sits where you want it to sit. If too much soil was removed, replace it on the unbalanced side. When the tree looks just right, cut off all dead-looking roots.

You must place fresh soil under the roots. Push this soil down on top of the roots and move the tree a little to make certain the fresh soil mixture and roots are making contact. This is a hard place to push in the soil so examine carefully.

Add soil and press down firmly with your hands.

Use chopsticks to push soil close around roots.

Five months later—the little tree is now well established.

Push down with your hand and then use the narrow stick to make certain the soil touches all parts of the roots. You may have to repeat this procedure three or four times. When your hands feel the compactness of the roots and soil, go around the edge of the container pushing in the soil. When you are sure all edges are even and compact, water your plant well. Put it in a shady place for at least two weeks.

In a nursery: would you buy this tree?

This little tree has excellent possibilities. The roots are already adjusted to grow-ing in the small space of a gallon can. The structure of the tree itself offers in-teresting possibilities for training.

Actually, buying a good miniature tree is not so difficult. Whatever the tree you choose—pine, juniper, maple, or cypress—look for a tree with an interesting shape and then try to consider all the possibilities of its arrangement in a container. This small tree offers many possibilities. What sort of container would you select for it?

In a container: you see a landscape

Here is a sample of what you can do by just planting in the container. Your own touch can create an unusual and yet *natural* effect. Here the little tree is planted in the right hand corner. A huge boulder (size—three inches!) goes in the center with gravel sprinkled lightly around—a scene created as if by nature.
What happens? Suddenly this isn't a plant in a pot—not at all. It is a landscape in miniature.

What to do
with a large cedar

We call this a large cedar only because it comes from the nursery in a five-gallon can and is 25 inches tall. Ordinarily, such a tree would not be considered the best material for bonsai.

When planting such a cedar follow the same rules as for a smaller tree, remembering that a larger tree requires a larger container if it is to live. You must also give careful attention to balancing your tree in its container.

Use your pruning shears and copper wire to give the tree the desired shape. Here we are attempting to bring some of the branches in toward the lower trunk. This must be done gradually, using your own good judgment.

To the left is a cedar as it came from the nursery. Heavy watering produced too many branches and a crowded effect. Cut and bend back the top of the can so that trunk and root may be seen. Prune and wire to the desired shape. In this case it is better to wire before removing from the can because there is less chance of disturbing the root.

Your cedar, pruned, wired and transplanted in its new container. Be sure to water well before transplanting. For a later repotting in a smaller container, prune top and roots again.

Place your tree where you decide it looks best in the container.

How to use a container without holes

A container without holes is not usually recommended for miniature trees, but it can be used by following the same principles already described.

Leave one corner of the container free of gravel and soil, as shown at top left. Cover the remainder of the bottom of the container with gravel and add a layer of mixed soil.

The reason for the bare corner in the container is to supply air and let you know when there is enough water.

Put in mixed soil.

Press soil down firmly with your hands.

Use a stick to help get the soil down deep among roots. Add more soil and pack down well.

Your little tree is finished now and ready for watering. Keep it in the shade, sheltered from the wind.

Add rocks and driftwood.

After two months and some judicious pruning, notice the change. Moss can be added at any stage you prefer.

After four months, give the tree a real pruning.

Surplus water comes out here.

Pyracantha: it is most adaptable

The pyracantha always comes in a shape naturally adaptable to miniature development. Most trees have a distinctive style of growth; nature helps you create the shape you wish. In this pyracantha we have followed the natural shape of the tree in pruning to the shape we want. Pyracanthas are widely available and not high in price.

False cypress: proportions are good

This lovely little tree (*Chamalcyparis pisifera*) is only 4 inches high yet it still resembles a normal tree because of its proportions. In the nursery you have a wide choice of any particular type of tree within one price range. Price is determined by the size of the can or pot and the rarity, not the shape of the tree. Therefore, search for an attractive natural shape in buying your tree.

Use driftwood and rock for an aged effect

The pine is a Japanese favorite for miniature treatment, but it is not always easy to find suitable pines in this country. Even when you are fortunate enough to find the right pine it may be expensive. A pine is a marvelous subject however; if you collect little trees you probably will want one. Since the miniature pine will grow for many years, you can look forward to added charm and interest as it ages. Driftwood and rock will help you to create the effect of age.

Owner: Harold Iwamasa

Volcanic rock suggests a mountain cliff

Here we are following nature. The volcanic rock, representing a cliff, gives a feeling of massiveness. The tree, placed next to the rock, gives the illusion of a huge tree towering far above the cliff.

In the future, when the moss grows over the rock, it will add to the impression of great age.

The volcanic rock is soft; we were able to dig a hole and plant a second tiny tree in the top of the rock.

Irish yew: a good tree to keep small

The point to study here is that all branches grow close together. Over and over you have seen this effect in trees growing freely and naturally, yet this little Irish yew is only 14 inches tall.

Juniper: always an interesting form

Junipers seem to assume an interesting shape naturally. We have used the same type of container for both the yew on the opposite page and the juniper below, yet both are well balanced. Some junipers grow naturally in many different directions at once, not just in a single direction. Confusion? Not at all—just the natural growth of the tree. Junipers are widely stocked in nurseries and are usually reasonable in price.

Bargain: it cost less than $1.00

Some of the best miniature plants are also nursery bargains. I liked this variegated weigela for its white bordered leaves; obviously it would make a different looking arrangement in another container. I paid the nurseryman about 95 cents.

Owner: George Ishikawa

Bargain: it cost less than $1.50

In a gallon can at the nursery, this nerium seemed uninteresting. We tried planting it in a tall container and achieved the interesting result you see here. The
main effect is one of asymmetrical balance. The plant reaches out to one side,
balancing the height and weight of the container.

A small nursery-grown cedar.

Look what happened . . .

At the nursery you can find almost any size and variety of tree. In the nursery container the roots are already bound.

Your project is to preserve the basic natural shape of your nursery-grown tree. On these pages we show what you can do with a small nursery-grown cedar. The branches of these trees are very flexible, especially in springtime when they are growing. This makes them easy to wire and shape.

Usually, the distance from the top of the nursery container to the soil level is

Plant sidewise to make design more interesting.

...to this cedar in half an hour

about 2 or 3 inches; this facilitates watering in the nursery. Inside the container you will find leaves and moss and grass. Therefore, you cut the can as shown in the photographs, bending it back so that you can examine the trunk base.

Next you decide what type of container you will use. You prepare your mixed soil and you prepare the container to receive the tree.

Decide roughly how you want to plant your tree. In this case, notice the tree is put in slanting toward the left. Couldn't the trunk really bend more gracefully than it does naturally? Of course it could! All that's needed is to wire loosely, starting from the base of the trunk and working up. Wire should always spiral to the left.

As you wire, if you see a branch you don't want, cut it off. Gently bend the tree and wire to suggest the shape you want. Doing so, you will see if the wire is strong enough and will hold. Wait until you have finished transplanting before bending to the final shape you want.

Now wire the side branches and trim off those you don't want. Wait until you have transplanted to finish pruning the main branches and to finish bending. Cut down the can, removing the tree and soil. Use a stick to remove half of this soil. Prune the dead-looking roots and then plant the tree slanting to the left.

Anchor one end of the wire deep in the soil near the root and coil the rest loosely around the trunk.

Bend the tree to the shape you want, pruning off overgrowth.

The leaning cedar has a reposeful quality.

Now finish the bending and pruning to the shape you have in mind. Be careful not to move the main root or attached soil. Grasp the bottom of the trunk with one hand and place the other hand about two inches higher up, then bend the trunk gently until you have achieved the shape you want. Follow the same procedure in shaping the branches. Now finish trimming. Water well and keep in the shade.

Use wire only where
you wish to change form

Even though the wire shows, do not worry about it. From a distance no one will
notice it (see above photo), and before very long the wire will have done its
job and you can take it away. Notice in the close-up on the right how little
wiring is actually needed to draw the two main branches together.

Owner: George Ishikawa

How to limit the height of your maple

Our plan here was to give the maple a spreading form and also to keep the tree at about the same height. Notice how we used wire loosely woven around the trunk to shape and shorten the tree.

After eight or twelve months we removed the wire. The tree was then in its dormant period and it had taken on the desired shape.

Even fast-growing plants are worth a try

Experiment with plants. Here is a fast-growing shrub with shiny leaves, the mirror plant (*Coprosma*). It is not considered by most miniature growers to be a suitable dwarf subject at all. Give it a try, though, if you find a likely one. You may be surprised at the results! Again notice the use of wire in shaping.

The gnarled trunk is the attraction

Here is a really fine miniature holly, which now and then can use a bit of wire
to keep it in shape.

Note the large, gnarled trunk and moss-grown roots, which give the impression
of old age.

The weeping branches are the attraction

This kind of evergreen, the Atlantic (blue) cedar, can take a lot of bending. Here we have achieved a "weeping" effect. The grass adds interest to the scene. Note how the wiring has been done on this tree. It is loosely wound around the trunk, secured at the given spot, and brought over to bend the branches into their curved positions.

Here are two mountainside junipers

Two junipers brought down from the mountains are pictured here. Both are likely bonsai subjects although they couldn't be more different in form.

The overhanging effect and the exposed roots of the juniper above give the impression of great age.

This straight growing juniper suggests a forest giant. It still requires a bit of wire to give it a "natural" appearance.

With a heavy single trunk

This 9-inch holly bonsai has a mushroom-shaped top, a marvelous thick trunk, and moss-covered topsoil. In its simply designed round container, what landscape situation does it suggest to you?

With a heavy double trunk

Here is a miniature tree that spreads two "wings" far out beyond its container. Notice how small this container is in comparison with the large double trunk of the tree.

Do you wonder how such a large tree can live in such a tiny container? Careful pruning of leaves and roots is the answer.

The Japanese call these tiny arrangements *mame bonsai*. (In Japanese, "mame" means "little bean"). Other growers just call them baby bonsai. You can see how small these trees are by comparing the scale of the tiny maple and the cigarette lighter on page 90.

Cultivation of *mame bonsai* is a wonderful hobby. It is fun to see how small a tree you can grow, and still give it a natural shape.

The care and planting of a tiny tree in a very small container is the same as for other miniature trees, but you have to be more careful every step of the way. It is important to have near-perfect drainage. Because you have very little soil, you must water more often. You must feed them very small amounts of fertilizer, but again more often.

To keep your *mame bonsai* tiny, you must prune and pinch frequently.

These little trees are called "Baby Bonsai"

Almost any tiny tree will do for your *mame bonsai* arrangement. Look at these insignificant nursery plants—and the splendid results you can achieve with them. On the facing page, the tallest tree in the top photograph is 6 inches high; in the middle photograph, 4 inches high; in the bottom photograph, just 5 inches.

Pictured below is all the material you will need.
Cover the hole with broken pot, line the bottom of the container with gravel, and then add a little mixed soil.
Place your tree in the desired spot, add the soil as before and press down.
Put driftwood in behind tree.

How to arrange a miniature maple

Bring the
little tree
indoors

Below is the new baby bonsai, with rocks and Irish moss added. To the right, you see what can happen in just eight weeks. The little maple has filled out and assumed its proper importance in the arrangement.

Owner: Norma Jean Johnson

After your tiny arrangement is finished, water well and keep it in the shade. Such a tree must be kept moist at all times and it requires plenty of fresh air. After it has remained in the shade for a few days, you may bring it inside. Place it on the sunny side of the room where it will be exposed to daylight and sunshine. The leaves always grow toward the light. The tree is young and will adjust to its given place. If the tree starts looking weak, move it back outside for awhile. Miniature arrangements like this one make wonderful window decorations.

A Hawaiian fern root container

The Hawaiian fern root, used commercially as a support for the vine type of indoor plant, makes a good container for baby bonsai. You can easily cut it to the proper size and it makes an ideal growing place for your plant.

Hollow out a space large enough to accommodate the root of your tree, place the tree inside, and add soil mix as instructed before. Neither drain hole nor fertilizer is necessary.

Anything planted in the fern root should thrive, if you give the needed care.

A pine tree, 1 inch high and two years old, started from seed. Patience is the keynote if you start your miniature from seed. While it grows you can be planning its future shape and experiencing the added delight of bringing your tree up from the beginning.

Japanese maple, 3 inches high and two years old. You can place such a *bonsai*, planted in fern root, in a dish. By putting water in the dish you can keep your plant well watered. The fern root will deliver the proper amount of moisture up to your tree.

Baby bonsai: pine

This five-year-old pine is just 6 inches tall. Notice how it has branched out and achieved a form suggesting a full-sized tree.

Baby bonsai: maple

Here is a 6-inch maple. A rock has been added to make the tiny arrangement more natural. Cover the container in the photograph with your hand and see if you have not observed a similar scene.

Owner: Manuel Quan

Little tree: grown from seed

This black pine was planted from seed in February, 1946, and photographed in April, 1955. In our photograph it is only 6 inches tall.

To develop and keep such a tiny miniature you need a small container, soil that is not too rich, and enough devotion to inspect your little tree and give it the care it needs.

Not a tree: a miniature ivy

There are several dozen varieties of ivy. Many of them do nicely as miniatures. In making your own selection, keep to one of the smaller leafed varieties. This little ivy is ten years old and just 6 inches tall. The root exposed against a rock gives the effect of an aged tree.

A tiny juniper — a tiny cedar

If you like more colorful containers, you have an added reason for trying the very small miniatures. These little fellows seem to combine more happily with decorative containers than bigger miniatures.

The two small trees here are 6 inches tall and both are five years of age. Yet because of the natural characteristics of the two, the juniper on the left has already assumed the shape of the bonsai while the cedar will require more time.

A tiny Japanese boxwood

Boxwood, by its nature, is quite easily cared for. It is one of the exceptions to many of the general precautions stated earlier. It may be placed in the sun or in the shade and it may also be brought inside.

Here two boxwoods have grown to make one bonsai. This tiny boxwood is 6 inches tall. It will keep its shape indefinitely, except that the trunks will grow larger.

Ideas from everyday living

When you decide to create a scene— of a garden, landscape, jungle or meadow—
you must first have in mind a fairly clear idea of the effect you are aiming for.
Perhaps without your realizing it, everyday living has taught you what is natural
looking, what isn't, what is in proportion, what is not. This teaching will help
when you start picking materials. But before the materials, you must work out
your idea. No matter what you decide upon—a pasture, a hillside, a house and
garden under a tree, or a woodland scene—you will want it to look quite natural.

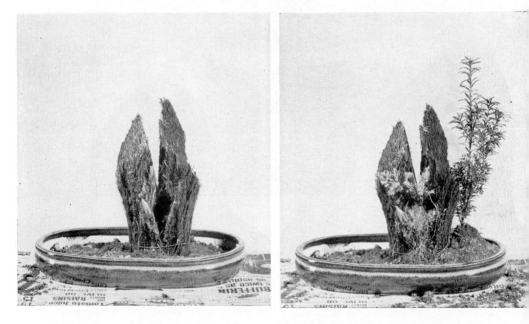

Place the fern root off-center in the container. Here we used two pieces of it. Notice the wire
holding them together, and the hole in the middle of the fern root.

Start your planting with the tallest tree. The yew is placed in position and the juniper is planted in the hole of the fern root. Next plant the boxwood, the tiny cedar and add the rock. Last come the small pine tree and more rocks.

Back view of the scene as it is being arranged.

Back view with another juniper and more rocks. The back view should also be interesting.

When you have decided on your subject, first pay attention to the main object around which the scene will be built. Only then pick out your container, choose your smaller trees, decide on secondary material.

There are no set rules, of course, except that you enjoy yourself and end up satisfied with your handiwork. If you already have something on hand you want to use, start with that. Anything you like that will give your miniature arrangement a natural look is satisfactory.

The arrangement almost completed. Use moss and baby tears to fill in bare spots and to grow up to the fern root.

Jungle scene

Lush jungle life is certainly suggested here. It came about—first, by a few well chosen materials; next, care in the selection of the container; last and most important, the work of the creative imagination to give us a natural effect. Fern root was used for the moss to grow on. These carefully selected trees—pine, boxwood, juniper, cedar and yew—blend into this jungle scene. Rocks and other secondary material such as baby tears and moss give the finished product a thick, dense appearance.

When photographed, this completed arrangement was four months old.

Miniature garden: under an elm

Notice the size of tree and the size of the house. This relationship is the dramatic thing here. Rock, baby tears, moss and grass are the working ingredients in this landscape. Without them, the elm would not be so interesting.

Miniature garden: on a rock ledge

It is quite possible to carve or whittle a bit of soft volcanic rock to make a stone house like this one. Use hammer and chisel, or if you wish, get a set of simple sculptor's tools. Build your scene around the house. Here, two kinds of trees are used: maple and cypress.

The tiny figure of the man and a two-story carved house set the scale. The size of the rock is in harmony with the small tree behind it, a three-inch maple. The scene changes as the maple gets its new leaves in spring, colors change in autumn, leaves fall away in winter.

The 7-inch cypress looks as natural as any tree you may see growing in a neighbor's garden. Baby tears cover this miniature hillside.

Miniature garden: in the country

The house and the tiny fence plus the various sized rocks gives this six-inch juniper height plus width, and give the whole arrangement its feeling of naturalness. Here is a country scene; here is nostalgia and remembrance. The possibilities in miniature gardens of this sort are just about endless.

Miniature garden: lofty tree, little bridge

If this 12-inch spruce were in a container by itself, it would not seem to be a large tree. Yet in this scene, between two 5-inch cypresses, it obviously has the look of a giant tree. One cypress was planted in front of the rocks, one behind the rocks. The 2-inch shrub planted in front to the right is there to make the spruce look even larger. Moss covers the soil. With the tiny bridge added, you can picture a brook murmuring its way along.

Miniature landscape: in the mountains

The way the rocks are placed around this 8-inch tree leaves little doubt that we are looking on a sturdy mountain scene. The small plants on the right have a special role to play. Their assignment is to make the central tree seem even taller and more rugged.

If the trees were in the container alone, with no rocks, no house, no fence, no tiny dogs, you would sense a great difference. This is a less disciplined but more inviting opportunity to create not an abstraction but a small piece of the living, peopled world.

Miniature landscape: on a ranch

Notice the green grass hanging over the edge of the container. Notice how two different sized pieces of driftwood are carefully placed, as are the small rocks. There the stallion stands under the tree, in the shelter of the smaller piece of driftwood. Here we are looking at a windy canyon, which might be on a Colorado or Wyoming ranch.

Use moss to complete the scene

Above you see a maple and a juniper intermingling their branches. In nature, you often see trees of different species growing intimately. We are suggesting such a situation in our photograph.

The two trees are planted in a hollow piece of volcanic rock. The moss growing over the edge looks natural; the small figure under the juniper suggests some human participation in this scene.

On the opposite page a five-year-old black pine grows out of neatly planted moss. The grass in front of the rock creates a note of naturalness and of age.

Moss likes water. If you can manage to keep your moss fresh and green, then you will know that you are giving your bonsai good care.

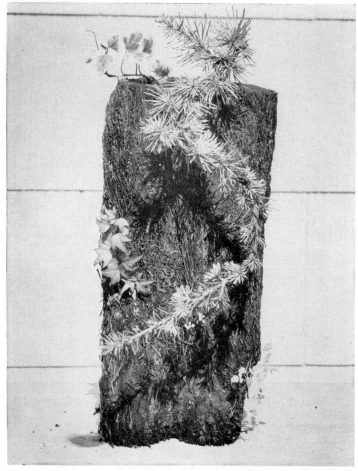

Owner: Ben Kunisawa

Hawaiian fern root is a handy material

Florists' shops and nurseries sell fern root in almost any size you might want. This is a soft material, easy for you to cut it into almost any desired shape.

Here a twelve-inch-high fern root has been planted to give the effect of a cliff side. In the top you see a five-year-old cedar trained with wire to grow down the side.

Ivy and fern have been planted in the sides of the fern root simply by digging a small hole with a kitchen knife, inserting the root, and making it firm with a small amount of soil. If you wish, you can place the whole fern root in a shallow dish when displaying it inside the house.

Two small cedars planted in fern root suggest two trees growing on top of a hill. Since the fern root itself is in a container, you need only to put water in that container and to sprinkle the tree now and then with water to wash away dust.

Fern root offers almost endless possibilities. Let your own imagination lead you into quite original ideas with this versatile material.

Owner: Ben Kunisawa

The finished product. In a short time, all the green trees and shrubs will grow and this will become a hillside scene.

With fern root, a hillside garden scene

Fern root has many of the good qualities of fine soil; because of this almost any plant will grow in it. You can grow trees in and around a piece of fern root and use moss and perhaps roots to fill in the bare spots.

In a fern root arrangement, all sides can be equally interesting.

Here is the same arrangement from the back.

Steady your piece of fern root so that it will hold a tree or two. Small rocks at the top help to hold the soil and to give a more natural effect. Next, plant your trees in the pockets dug in the fern root.

Place rocks and plant some boxwood in the container. Turn your arrangement around and plant a yew. Pack down all your mixed soil and then plant moss so that it will grow up to cover the base of the fern root.

Container inside a container

Here an elm has been planted in fern root and the fern root in turn placed in a container. Moss, grass, rocks and the small figure all contribute to the impression of reality. The fern root suggests a small bluff above a meadow.

The natural containers — working together

Here we have a maple with three trunks, which we want to show off. To do so
we have built a stage of fern root.

The fern root sits in a piece of concave volcanic rock and the right side is built
up with soil to produce an asymmetrical design. Baby tears are planted at the base
of the fern root and a bit of grass is put in at the left to soften the whole effect.
Many nurseries can supply soft volcanic rock for arrangements of this kind.

A white fir—a black pine

Above you see a white fir with the soil built up unevenly to suggest a hill. The moss over all gives the effect of grass. The light-colored rock near the base of the tree provides an interesting note of contrast.

On the right is a foot-tall black pine planted in fern root, covered with fast growing baby tears, providing a perfect setting for the tiny Oriental house.

Cover the container with your hand. Do you have the feeling of being high in the mountains viewing a house hanging on the edge of a cliff?

Miniature garden: a farmstead

The tall tree is eight inches high; the cypress below measures five inches. Notice how rocks are partially concealed by the plant materials below.

In arrangements like this one you can create almost any scene you like. This is a farmyard; would you prefer to suggest a small city garden, a corner in a park, a patio or terrace, a country lane? All you need is the idea, and imagination to devise the elements that will give your natural stage its sense of reality.

Miniature garden: a quiet pool

This four-inch spruce grows slantwise under the rock at right to give the impression of hanging over a pool. This impression is carried out further by covering the topsoil with polished stones, such as are found in the bottom of a river or a creek. Actually, there is no free water here. But don't you get the cool impression of a pool?

We used stones of different colors, added the two tiny cranes—all to set a beautiful stage for the lovely miniature spruce.

Miniature landscape: a meadow

It doesn't matter what you call it: bonsai, dwarf tree, miniature tree, miniature garden. The idea is to suggest a natural scene in small proportion.

Here a thirteen-inch redwood, an interesting rock, the tiny figure of a cow and some moss are all that were needed to depict a meadow in miniature.

Miniature landscape: a roadside

You have been driving all morning; you are tired. There it is beside the road—a tree leaning away from the hill, throwing its shade, inviting you to stop and sit for a while, stretch your legs, relax. That's what our scene suggests. Actually the tree is not 40 feet high, it is 10 inches high. These boulders are pebbles. The landscape is only a miniature. But look how inviting it can be!

Elm, fern root, container and tiny maple—all ready for planting. Note the white gravel in two places on the fern root. Place the fern root in the container. Be sure that it is firm and will not move.

The elm is removed from the can and ready for planting on the back of the fern root. In this case, the elm is actually planted in the container.

Plant the maple on the fern root, then plant grass on the left and place rocks near the elm and the maple. Sprinkle soil around the fern root and pack it down firmly in the container.

Note: Moss will grow almost anywhere you want it to grow. Only precaution: water it well.

More ideas for fern root

Elm, maple, grass, moss . . . here all are growing in fern root, this simple material which is adaptable for so many purposes, especially for creating an aged-looking arrangement.

Fern root is popular because of the excellent results almost invariably obtained. Fern root as a planter is practically foolproof; it offers just what most plants like as a growing medium. Because it is soft enough for roots to penetrate yet firm enough to keep its shape, you can use it in place of soil.

Fern root is particularly useful in miniature tree cultivation because it permits you to build the soil level above the rim of the container. In this respect it often is more satisfactory than rocks or driftwood.

Two ways to use bamboo

There are many different bamboos suitable for miniature arrangement. Here we have used a miniature variety, placing it offcenter in a shallow container.

Large or small, bamboo has its own style of growing. If you use it, try to emphasize its natural qualities in your living composition.

The bamboos are quite easy to care for. They like lots of water, a clay-type soil, quite damp.

How do you like the arrangement on the opposite page? Whatever your artistic nature, abstract compositions are fun. Here the bamboo is growing through the sides of the fern root.

Hollow the piece of fern root, leaving a thin shell. Then put in your bamboo plant and fill hole with soil as usual. The shoots will grow out through all sides of the fern root. It is a good idea to plant moss around the base of the fern root.

This miniature was just planted

This nerium came from the nursery in a gallon can. The plant's height and shape suggested the type and size of container used.

In a year or two this miniature will be as interesting as the one you see on the opposite page.

This miniature is four years old

Here two elms are planted on fern root, with uneven rocks and baby tears.
Together the two elms have the balanced shape of a miniature tree, but the unusual rocks and the moss are essential to complete the scene.

Bird's-nest cypress

This little bird's-nest cypress is ten years old and 10 inches tall. While not old compared to many typical Japanese bonsai, it does show its years of good care. In this case the shape and appearance of the bonsai takes precedence over age. This bonsai does not require transplanting because its leaves are green and fresh looking. When the leaves begin to lose their freshness, transplanting time is at hand. Notice, however, that the soil is beginning to rise above the edge of the container. In this miniature the soil was purposely arranged as you see it.

Oceanside cypress

Here is a more venerable bonsai—fifty years old, 18 inches tall. It suggests a
full-grown tree such as you might see in a park or rough hillside near the ocean.
Actually, neither age nor height is as important as the fact that it looks natural,
like a miniature equivalent of a mature tree growing naturally.

It took years of proper care to produce this fine bonsai. If the bonsai idea catches
on with you, someday you may own a collection of fine old trees like this one.

Owner: Norma Jean Johnson

The ginkgo
with the beautiful leaves

The ginkgo is one of the trees most favored by the bonsai cultivator. It is easy to keep it in the desired shape by pruning.

The bonsai above is 17 inches high and only two years old.

Compare it with the thirty-year-old ginkgo at the right. Several small trees were planted together and twisted to produce this interesting 20-inch bonsai.

Even the colorful Virginia creeper can make a good miniature subject.

Vine and fruit tree miniatures

Almost any growing plant is good material for a bonsai. The fast-growing, color-ful Virginia creeper at left is 13 inches high and ten years old. It is easy to prune to take different shapes.

You can grow a good miniature olive tree if you wish. The 21-inch tree above bears fruit and is a good example of what the Japanese call chokkan-style bonsai.

From the high mountains

Growing in the high mountains, the black pine is one of the favorites of collectors. This tree has difficulty adjusting to new surroundings because its natural locale is at very high altitude. Even though it requires a little more care, many miniature tree collectors think it well worth their while.

From the open field

Taken straight from a country field, this dead trunk with a single living branch makes an intriguing miniature subject. The trunk gives the appearance of a large piece of driftwood or a big, gnarled root. The green leaves contrast with the dead wood.

You can make your own discoveries

Keep your eyes open for different, unusual shapes. If you see something that attracts your attention do not be afraid to gather it for a miniature arrangement. If you watch closely, you are quite likely to happen upon many beauties in fields or mountains.

The huge, dead-looking trunk on this wisteria, 14 inches high, is the attention-catcher here. The branches grow out of the back with the green leaves making a fine foil.

This plum tree was cut to the ground near its roots and left to die. A miniature tree fancier discovered it and made this unusual composition. The exposed roots and unusual position of the trunk attain a beautiful balance.

Everybody's favorite — the Japanese maple

This little 17-inch maple is fifteen years old. The Japanese maple, although a native of Japan, has long been a favorite garden tree in America where it is widely available. The tree in the photograph is a good example of miniature tree culture in the Japanese style. It was grown, however, in the United States.

The pistachio—a good subject

If this tree were a pine or maple you might think it was a Japanese bonsai. However, the Japanese don't grow the pistachio as a miniature potted tree. This beautiful tree was grown in California by Dick Geisreiter, an American.

An ancient: seventy-five-year-old elm

This 20-inch elm is seventy-five years old. Trees of this type are favorites of bonsai collectors. Such experts look for large trunks with a rough texture and check the size of the leaves in proportion to the trunk and tree form. This old elm looks as natural in its container as a large elm would look in the back yard.

Another ancient: ninety-five-year-old pomegranate

Here is an example of the finest bonsai you will ever see. It meets all the requirements—large, rough trunk surmounted by perfectly proportioned leaves and branches. This 22-inch-high pomegranate is ninety-five years old.

America: a grove of young elms

Here is a beautiful example of an American bonsai. Imagination plus a feeling for reality combined these five elms in a shady grove. Cover the container with your hand and it would be difficult to tell that the trees were not growing naturally in a farmer's field.

Japan: a most ancient azalea

This is the ultimate in bonsai. It is a 30-inch-high, 265-year-old azalea.
If you start now, perhaps your great-great-great-great-grandson can own such a
plant and reflect on the five generations of gardeners who shaped it with lov-
ing care.